zen 24/7

zen 24/7

ALL ZEN/ALL THE TIME

PHILIP TOSHIO SUDO

HarperSanFrancisco
A Division of HarperCollins*Publishers*

Grateful acknowledgment is given to the following for permission to include excertps from previously published works as well as original material:

Poems from Crow With No Mouth © 1989 by Stephen Berg. Reprinted by permission of Copper Canyon Press, Post Office Box 271, Port Townsend, WA 98368.

Wild Ways: Zen Poems of Ikkyu © 1995, translated and edited by John Stevens. Reprinted by arrangement with Shambhala Publications, Inc., Boston.

New Lao Tzu © 1995, by Ray Grigg. Reprinted by permission of Charles E. Tuttle Co., Inc., of Boston, Massachusetts, and Tokyo, Japan.

Peace is Every Step © 1991, by Thich Nhat Hanh. Reprinted by permission of Bantam Books, Inc., New York.

HarperCollins books may be purchased for educational, business, or sales promotional use. For information please write: Special Markets Department, HarperCollins Publishers, 10 East 53rd Street, New York, NY 10022.
HarperCollins Web site: http://www.harpercollins.com

HarperCollins®, 💾®, and HarperSanFrancisco™ are trademarks of Harper-Collins Publishers, Inc.

FIRST EDITION
Designed by Joseph Rutt

Library of Congress Cataloging-in-Publication Data
Sudo, Philip Toshio
Zen 24/7 : All Zen All the Time / Philip Toshio Sudo.— 1st ed.
p. cm.
Includes bibliographical references
ISBN 0–06–251678–7 (alk. Paper : paper)
1. Religious life—Zen Buddhism. I. Title.
BQ9286 .S83 2000
294.3'444—dc21   00–050554
01 02 03 04 05 RRD (H) 10 9 8 7 6 5 4 3 2 1

To my mother and father, who live within me 24/7

contents

INTRODUCTION

Any and every action can be a source of insight—even enlightenment—whether it's toothbrushing, going to the bathroom, or opening a can of beer. That's the promise of zen.

No matter what we do or where we go, zen is available to us 24/7: twenty-four hours a day, seven days a week. It never goes away, no matter how routine the day may seem. The most mundane details of life contain zen's profound truths, if we're of the mind to look for them.

It's easy to find significance in those days that rise above the ordinary—a graduation, some great athletic or career triumph, a wedding, the birth of a child. But what about all the days in between? The aim of *Zen 24/7* is to look at the everyday, ordinary parts of our lives and see the meaning in them, too; to become so absorbed in the commonplace that we come to know a deeper reality. In so doing, we make today—plain old today—a truly special day.

Zen teaches that our approach to today determines our whole approach to life. The Japanese call this attitude

Ichi-nichi issho: "Each day is a lifetime." We arise in the morning newly born. As we pass through the day, we age and gain experience. When we tire at day's end, we "die" and take our rest. That one arc serves as a miniature of our entire life. What we do during a single day—and how we do it—becomes the foundation of our whole lifetime. For what is life but the sum of our days?

This very day can be a life's turning point. In a single moment, we can decide to walk the path that has no end.

Starting now.

Let the day begin.

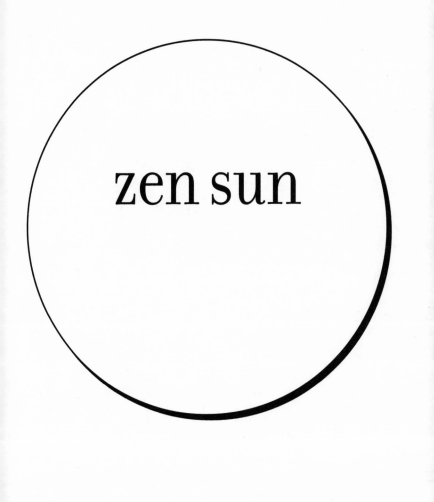

zen
rise and shine

alarm clock
breath
shaving
toothbrushing
blinds

zen alarm clock

Much as we may want to roll over and go back to sleep, we have to start the day sometime. Whatever serves to stir us from our slumber—the alarm clock, the light from outside, the dog's cold nose—remember: The purpose of zen is to do the same.

We all need to awaken, zen says—to our true nature, to the timeless essence at our core that connects us to everything and everybody. So many of us are spiritually asleep, oblivious to the precious gift we have. We take life for granted, sleepwalking until a shattering event knocks us awake. Zen says, don't wait until the car accident, the cancer diagnosis, or the death of a loved one to get your priorities straight. Do it now.

Let today's wake-up call signal the start of a new day—the first day of a new lifetime.

Awaken!

zen breath

Life begins with a single breath. The moment we're born and leave the womb of our mother, we start the lifelong process of inhale-exhale that continues until the moment we die. Nothing is more basic, more vital to our lives, than breathing. Yet rarely do we give it a thought.

A zen teacher once made that point dramatically before an assembled group of monks. The teacher asked, "What's the most important thing in life?"

"Food," said one.

"Work," said another.

"The pursuit of truth," said a third.

The teacher signaled for a monk to step forward. Grabbing the monk's head, he dunked it in a tub of water and held it down until the monk came up gasping for breath.

The assembly got the message: We can live days without food, years without work, or a lifetime without truth, but we cannot go more than minutes without a breath.

When you awake in the morning, stretch your arms to the sky and breathe deeply. Fill your insides with the emptiness around you.

Breathe easy. You're *alive*.

zen shaving

Shaving is like mowing the lawn. The moment we're finished, the growth starts coming back. Pretty soon we have to do it over all again.

The energy that makes our hair grow is the same that makes the grass grow. It's within us and around us. We're not separate from it; we're *of* it. It's right under our noses.

The zen master Wakuan is said to have challenged his students with the question, "Why has Bodhidharma no beard?" The question is a puzzle because the monk Bodhidharma is always shown with a beard.

Wakuan means for us to look inward—to look beneath outer appearances and see the energy that underlies all things. Bodhidharma may indeed have a beard, but that's just his physical form. The *essence* of Bodhidharma—the energy at his core, and the core of all of us—has no beard. That's the true Bodhidharma, and the true you and me. Don't identify with the outer form that grows the beard or the hair on the legs, Wakuan says, for it will one day die. Instead, identify *with the divine energy that makes the hair grow.* That goes on forever.

The truth cuts like a razor.

zen
TOOTHBrusHInG

No one thinks, "What a hassle, I have to brush my teeth *every morning for the rest of my life!*" We just brush our teeth in the morning. When the time comes to brush again, we brush again.

We learn the importance of daily brushing as children. Soon it becomes ingrained as a good habit, and we do it automatically.

Good habits are the building blocks of zen training. "Virtues are the fruit of self-discipline and do not drop from heaven of themselves as does rain or snow," says the zen master Zengetsu. Developing these good habits takes an attitude of *shugyo,* literally, "mastering one's deeds."

Some beginners get overwhelmed by the idea of *shugyo,* envisioning a narrow, straight line they have to walk for the rest of their days. They think, "What a long road ahead!" and become too daunted even to try. But the mind-set of *shugyo* should be as simple as brushing one's teeth.

No need to concern yourself with building a habit over time.

Just do it today.

zen
BLINDS

A zen story tells of the time the master Hogen prepared to give a lecture and pointed at the window blinds. In an instant, two monks went over and rolled them up.

Hogen watched the two and said, "The state of the first monk is good, not that of the other."

What Hogen observed was the state of mind each monk had in getting up and opening the curtains. Although the two monks had correctly perceived the master's wishes, zen scholars speculate that perhaps the second monk had moved out of a desire to curry favor with the teacher. In zen, there are no brownie points to be gained. One's actions either flow naturally from the heart or they do not. Even in opening the blinds, there is a zen way to proceed.

Along the same lines, an aikido instructor once described to me a test he took for promotion to the next level. Unbeknownst to him at the time, one-third of the test was determined by how he entered the hall and sat down *before his name was even called*. What the masters were looking for was whether the student was already in a continuous flow entering the hall, or whether he regarded the test as a separate point at which to "turn on" and impress the teachers.

When you open the blinds, open them like you're lifting the veil on enlightenment.

Or just open the blinds.

See?

zen
breakfast

doughnut
cup of coffee
cornflakes
morning news

zen
DOUGHNUT

In the go-go world of modern life, a lot of people think breakfast has to be fast—a doughnut on the way out the door with a cup of coffee in the car. But the very word *breakfast* has spiritual meaning.

To eat breakfast is, literally, to break one's fast—to resume eating after having an empty stomach. Never mind that the "fast" has been enforced by sleep. Just as deliberate fasting during the waking hours can be a means for spiritual renewal, so can the de facto fasting we do at night.

In zen monasteries, monks receive their meals with a chant reminding them of five things:

1. to be grateful of the meal, no matter how simple;

2. to appreciate the effort of all hands, both seen and unseen, who labored to put the food on the table;

3. to reflect on their own actions, and whether those actions make them deserving of the meal;

4. to regard the food as medicine to sustain their health and ward off illness;

5. to accept the meal as a means of attaining enlightenment.

When breaking the previous night's fast, we can start our day off the same way as those monks in the monastery: By putting our minds on the plane of gratitude before filling our empty stomachs.

In this way is breakfast indeed the most important meal of the day.

zen
CUP OF COFFEE

Wake up and smell the coffee?
  Smell the coffee and *wake up!*
  Zen.

zen
cornflakes

Before we fill our bowl with cornflakes, we should take a moment to look at the bowl empty. See it as a pair of hands cupped together.

According to legend, when Siddhartha Gautama departed on the journey that would lead to his enlightenment as Buddha, he took only a robe and an empty bowl. In the centuries to follow, zen masters symbolized their transference of authority by giving their successors a robe and a bowl.

Like hands cupped together, an empty bowl signifies a willingness to rely on the help of others. Such a bowl is always ready to receive, be it cereal or a pearl of wisdom.

Give thanks and be filled.

zen
morninɢ news

By definition, news is of the moment. But the din of daily events can so dominate our consciousness we forget that news and information aren't the same as wisdom. We may be up to the minute on the latest controversy, but as the *Tao Te Ching* teaches,

People who argue
do not understand;
And people who understand
do not argue.

Occasionally we go on vacation to a place where there are no newspapers and no television. And when we return we find the world hasn't ended. We realize that even though following the news may be essential to making a living, it has little to do with living a spiritual life. On the path of zen, we ultimately learn there's only one headline that matters: THE WAY TO ENLIGHTENMENT IS RIGHT HERE, RIGHT NOW.

See inside for details.

zen
GETTING DRESSED

clothes
makeup
hairstyle
mirror
smile

zen clothes

Everything we wear says something about us—how we see ourselves and want others to see us. Zen reminds us that the clothes don't make the man or woman. Underneath the outer trappings, we're all naked and divine.

Once, when the zen master Ikkyu was invited to a banquet, he showed up wearing his tattered traveling robe and straw hat. He was mistaken for a beggar and sent to the backdoor, where he was ushered away from the feast.

The next time he received an invitation, Ikkyu appeared in his ceremonial robes. Upon being served, he removed the robes and set them before his tray.

"What are you doing?" the host asked.

"The food belongs to the robes, not me," said Ikkyu on his way out the door.

We all don a uniform when we dress ourselves in the morning—even those people who wear the robes of zen monks. What does your dress say about you?

Whatever the message, remember: Beneath it all, we're of the same flesh.

Feel good in your skin.

zen makeup

Every face has its distinctive shape and features, but there are times we need to forget the face and remember that, in the end, we're nothing but dust and bones. So many of us agonize over our appearance, comparing ourselves unfavorably to models and movie stars, or even to the face of our youth, applying makeup to hide the lines or going under the knife to tighten the skin. But the zen master Ikkyu reminds us that, as ever, beauty is skin deep.

"Have a good look," he says. "Stop the breath, peel off the skin, and everybody ends up looking the same. No matter how long you live, the result is not altered.... Who will not end up as a skeleton?"

Once we come to grips with that fact, we realize that past the face, past the skeleton, lies our *honrai no memmoku:* Our original, primordial face—the face of the God-spirit within us all. As zen masters put it, "What was your face before your parents were born?" Hint: It's the God-face we show to the world every day.

The ad says, "Maybe she's born with it. Maybe it's Maybelline."

Zen says: She's born with it.

zen Hairstyle

There's nothing static about a head of hair. We may primp until our 'do looks just so or use sprays or gels to keep it in place, but even when set it's ever changing.

Every day, dozens of hairs fall out from shampooing and combing. Barring the onset of baldness, those hairs get replaced by new hair budding in the follicles, the way trees replenish their leaves.

Thus, every head of hair symbolizes the process of growth, death, and rebirth that's implicit in nature. Even though we can't see the change while it's in progress, it's happening before our eyes, in the same way that beneath the snow that covers the ground in winter lie the seeds of spring. A zen poem written in winter says,

sitting motionless, nothing happening—
spring coming, grass growing

How many times a day do we check our hair in the mirror? Each time we do, we're looking at a microcosm of nature's great cycles being played out right on top of our heads.

In zen, there are no bad hair days.

zen
mirror

Everything in this world—*everything*—is a reflection of Great Nature. As human beings, we're of the same energy source as all that surrounds us. Thus, when we look out at the world, we are nature gazing upon itself. Essentially, as Ikkyu says, all the world is a giant reflection of the same great force: "Mirror facing mirror—nowhere else."

Through zen training, we seek to become perfect mirrors—crystal clear reflections of nature and its processes. Zen masters refer to the ideal as *meikyo*, "spotless mirror" or "clear boundary." Keep polishing the mirror, they say, to see your reflection more clearly. No matter how long we train, new "dust spots" will always appear. We have to wipe those dust spots away before they obscure our vision. As the zen monk Shen-hsiu says,

This body is the tree of enlightenment,
The mind is like a bright mirror standing;
Take heed to always keep it clean,
And allow no dust to ever cling.

When we check the outer mirror to fix our hair, makeup, or clothes, we should remember to check our inner mirror, too. Before you look away from the mirror, remember to smile at yourself. Take a moment make sure the beauty *really* shines through.

Nature gazing at itself.

Lookin' good.

zen smile

What brings a smile to our face? It could be anything—a baby's gurgle, a dog greeting us at the door, eye contact with a handsome stranger. Whatever the case, a smile results from a part of ourselves enjoying a gift of nature.

Zen lore tells of a time the Buddha gathered his disciples for a speech, twirling a flower in his hand. As the audience sat silently, only one in the crowd, Kasyapa, was aware that the wordless sermon had already begun. Kasyapa broke into a broad smile at the master's message: All things reflect the divine energy of nature—every flower, every rock, every sound, every sight.

Once we realize that truth, we cannot help but smile.

zen
OUT THE DOOR

wristwatch
wallet
keys
door
stairs
good morning

zen wristwatch

The Hall of Fame baseball players Tom Seaver and Yogi Berra once shared the following exchange:

SEAVER: "What time is it?"
BERRA: "You mean now?"

No matter what time of day we check our watch, the only time is now. We may be running behind schedule, late for an appointment, or stuck in traffic, but we can't be anywhere other than where we are; our place in time cannot change. All we can do is make the best of each moment we're given.

"This day will not come again," says the zen master Takuan. "Each minute is worth a priceless gem."

With the hectic pace of modern life, many people live as though there aren't enough hours in the day. They cram their date books with appointments, working late into the night, living with a sense that the clock is always ticking. Other people, especially in their youth, live as though they have time in abundance, thinking they have a right to the future, that tomorrow is a given.

Life is always on the edge of death, one accident away. As the Japanese say of the future's uncertainty, "One inch ahead and all is total darkness." If we realize that truth, we begin to appreciate the time we have, however short it may be. We no longer feel driven to fill it up without stopping to reflect on our lives or fritter precious hours away in idle waste.

The only time and place to find enlightenment is in this moment.

No need to check your watch.

The time is now.

zen wallet

No one needs a wallet at home. A wallet is for when we venture into the larger world.

Typically, a wallet holds money, bank and credit cards, a driver's license, and some personal photos. Money enables us to buy goods and services; bank and credit cards give us access to more money without having to carry it; a driver's license establishes our identity in the world and allows us to move around; personal photos keep the protective spirit of loved ones close at hand while away from home.

Of course, the main thing that gets us through each trip into the world has nothing to do with what's in our wallet. Even should our wallet get lost or stolen, we still have to rely on our wits. Zen demands a spirit of self-reliance. "Need a fire? Best strike a flint," goes a zen saying. "Need water? Dig a well." Lose your money, you still have the means to live. Lose your identification, you still have your identity.

The key to security lies not in the money, the credit card, or the license.

It's in you.

zen
keys

For some reason, a lot of us have trouble remembering where we put our keys. Just when we're ready to leave the house on time, we end up having to search for our keys.

Zen demands attention to life's ordinary details—where we put things down, how we pick them up. In one single action, we can fall off the path or put ourselves back on. When mind and action are separate, zen is lost. We keep the two in sync by paying attention.

A zen story tells of a monk named Tenno who had just completed his apprenticeship to become a zen teacher. One rainy day, he went to visit the master Nan-in. As is customary in Japan, Tenno removed his shoes at the vestibule of the master's home.

Nan-in welcomed him in, and they sat down. After an exchange of greetings, the master said, "I was wondering, did you leave your umbrella on the left or the right of your shoes?"

The monk could not answer. Perhaps he had arrived with thoughts about what he wanted to say to his teacher or was nervous about the meeting. Perhaps he was thinking ahead to how his teacher would congratulate him on his promotion. In any event, Tenno had paid no attention to where he left his umbrella. Realizing he still lacked zen awareness, he put off teaching and resumed his apprenticeship.

When we put our keys down, we should be conscious of putting them down. When we pick them up, we should be conscious of picking them up. That's all there is to zen.

The best way to remember where we put things is to have a place for them. As the saying goes, "All things in their place, and a place for all things."

Therein lies the key.

zen
door

In the West, we're advised to "make an entrance" when we walk into a room. But in the art of the Japanese tea ceremony, that's impossible. The traditional houses used to host the events are purposely built with low doorways so that all who pass must bow their frames as they enter and exit. No one can stride through.

The intent is to physically impose a posture of humility, requiring the head to be down, and in so doing effect a change in attitude. Entering, one is humbled before the others present, as those who follow are humbled toward you; exiting, one is humbled before the outdoors and Great Nature.

The door to the teahouse thus symbolizes the only door that matters in life: the one leading to enlightenment. Step humbly through the door, with no expectations, into the great wide world. Find yourself there.

Open door, open mind.

zen
stairs

Ascending a long staircase brings to mind a zen saying, *Gojuppo hyappo:* "Fifty steps, one hundred steps."

Whenever we endeavor to learn something new in life, be it zen, a job, a sport, or a musical instrument, we should expect the process to take time and effort. *Gojuppo hyappo* means, if we've taken fifty steps up the staircase, see the effort through. Don't go halfway and stop. Take fifty more.

In so many ways, we quit at fifty steps. We take on a new hobby with a burst of enthusiasm, only to tire of it and move on to something else. We start a new diet, a new exercise program, a new relationship, and the moment things get hard we ditch it.

The truth of zen is, the staircase goes up step by step forever. There is never a top to reach for as long as we live. But we continue up the steps because the path is right, and *the process of climbing* is all that matters.

People get discouraged when they start looking too far ahead: "I can't make the climb, it's too high, so I'm not going to start." Or they commit today to taking a hundred steps every day and become disillusioned when, a week later, they haven't been able to keep up: "I can't stick to it, it's too big a commitment."

We needn't look any further ahead than today or commit to any more than taking one step. When we've taken one, we can commit to taking another. Pretty soon we've reached fifty. Pretty soon we've reached a hundred.

Pretty soon we've reached zen.

zen
GOOD MORNING

Whoever stops to think why we say "good morning"?

What makes a morning "good" is nothing more than our being alive.

How potent those words *good morning* can be if we truly believe them. Zen masters have a saying, *Hibi kore kojitsu:* "Every day is a good day." The Japanese word for *good* in this case, *ko,* consists of two characters placed side by side: the character for "woman" and the character for "child." How deep and good runs the love between a mother and child! That is the feeling with which zen masters instruct us to regard each day.

On a cosmic level, every day *is* a good day, no matter what difficulties or challenges may arise. If we fix that notion in our minds each morning, we will not allow ourselves to waste time in wallowing and self-pity: "Leave me alone, I'm having a bad day." Each day is a lifetime; so long as time remains, we can turn it around.

So often we exchange our morning pleasantries with words devoid of feeling.

Today, say "good morning" like you mean it.

zen JOB

commute
work
computer
phone ring
calendar
meeting
business card
handshake

zen commute

For many of us, the commute from home to work is a path so well traveled we can visualize the entire route in our minds—every signpost, toll booth clerk, and turn along the way. Yet each trip has its little variations. The weather changes; a construction project starts; a new billboard goes up. No matter how routine the commute seems, no two trips are ever the same.

Zen masters call that principle *ichigo ichie,* or "one time, one meeting." It began with the tea master Ii Naosuke, who served as chief administrator for the shogun in the nineteenth century. During that time, Naosuke faced the constant threat of assassination from political enemies. Thus, he began each morning with a cup of tea and the motto *ichigo ichie,* never knowing if that day's tea would be his last. His suspicions proved correct; he was assassinated in 1860. But his motto lives on in the Japanese tea ceremony. All who partake in the gathering recognize it as an unprecedented, unrepeatable experience. No matter how many times the ceremony gets performed, each one is a singular event, occupying a unique moment in time.

The same is true of our commute. We go and return, go and return, go and return.

Each trip is a once-in-a-lifetime experience.

zen work

Some people complain about their jobs, but zen says we should always be grateful for work; it's what puts a roof overhead and food on the table. A famous story tells of the master Hyakujo, who toiled around the temple grounds even at the age of eighty. His students pleaded with him to ease up, but he refused.

One day the students hid his tools to prevent Hyakujo from working. In turn, the master refused to eat.

"No work, no food," he said.

All of life is an interconnected system of work. Without the work of farmers, the food wouldn't grow. Without the work of truck drivers, it wouldn't get delivered. Without the work of grocers, it wouldn't get distributed. Everything that surrounds us—every building, every sidewalk, every object—is the result of human toil.

Like the monks in monasteries, we must learn to regard work as integral to our spiritual practice. That does not mean we have to devote ourselves to religious causes; it means we should approach work as a way to elevate our spirit. As the Japanese say, *Inoru yori kasege:* "Toil rather than pray."

No matter what our job title, no matter what our pay, we can choose to approach our work with dignity and care. In such a way can a pauper earn more respect than a president.

Put in an honest day's work. It is the building block of a spiritual life.

zen
computer

In this technological age, few machines have done more to change our lives than the computer. At times, those changes can be overwhelming. But dealing with change lies at the heart of zen study. If zen is to be an every-moment practice, then our time with the keyboard and mouse is part of that practice as well.

We can start our practice with one simple gesture: By nodding to the machine.

In the art of Japanese swordsmanship, the samurai bow to their swords before and after training as a way of showing reverence for the its power and significance in life.

By giving the computer a nod, we show similar respect for the power placed at our fingertips. Many of us depend on technology to make a living. By nodding to the computer, we recognize its contribution to our lives.

Nodding also thanks the unseen hands and minds who helped to create our machine. A computer is not born on a store's shelf. It comes from a line of scientists, engineers, inventors, programmers, mathematicians, designers, manufacturers—all of whom built on the knowledge of those who came before them. It comes from makers of plastics and glass, packers and shippers, workers who built the roads and rails and airplanes, their mothers and fathers who brought them into the world, and the teachers who taught them what they needed to know. The spirit of all of them exists in every machine. By nodding, we silently thank those people for what they gave to make the tool in front of us.

If we learn to show respect this way, an internal transformation takes place. The machine looks less soulless in our eyes. We become aware of the interplay between tool and user and start to recognize the interconnectedness—the oneness—of all things.

From there we adopt the attitude of nodding toward *everything*—the lamp, the desk, the roof, and the floor. Soon, we're living a life full of gratitude.

From one simple nod do we change with a changing world.

zen
PHONE RING

Why is it that when the phone rings, we become Pavlovian dogs? We drop everything we're doing to pick up the phone.

A zen lesson applies here from the master Ummon. One morning he saw a monk responding obediently to a monastery bell that signaled the time to don ceremonial robes. "The world is vast and wide," Ummon said. "Why do you put on your seven-piece robe at the sound of a bell?"

Ummon was asking, Are you answering the bell out of habit, because that's what you're supposed to do? Or is it because that's what you *want* to do?

Instead of being a slave to the bell, Ummon says, let it remind us to put thought behind our actions. When we respond to the bell, we should do so aware of our inherent freedom. In the grand scheme of things, we have control over whether we answer it or not.

Before picking up the phone, pause a moment and let it ring one more time. Don't answer the phone in mid-ring; let the full ring complete itself—and listen to it—

before picking up the receiver. In that moment, compose yourself.

Note the difference. Those who answer the phone in obedience say, "Hello?"

Those who answer in control say,

"Hello."

zen
calendar

Zen masters have a saying, *Sanchu rekijitsu nashi:* "No calendar in the mountain monastery." Imagine there were no calendar. No days of the week, no months, no years. How would we orient ourselves in time? In the same way as the ancients: Through the rise and fall of the sun each day, the cycle of the moon each month, the cycle of the seasons each year. The more we attune ourselves to that timeless rhythm, the closer we live to nature.

We rely on concepts such as "Monday" and "February" to organize our complex schedules and mark the passage of time. But we should remember the monk in the monastery, who regards the past and future as an illusion. To the monk, there is no yesterday or tomorrow; there is only this moment.

Twenty-four hours a day.

Seven days a week.

Three hundred sixty-five days a year.

zen
meeting

Meetings are a fact of working life. They can also be an incredible waste of time. We can sit for hours listening to unfocused leaders or people who talk just to hear their own voice, and come away with nothing accomplished.

In zen, it is a cardinal sin to waste time. To waste time is to squander the here and now, which, if you think about it, is all that we have.

It is bad enough for us to waste our own time. To waste the time of others is even worse. When people show a lack of respect for our time, it is rude; to show the same lack of respect toward others is not only rude, it violates our spiritual practice.

If we're going to call a meeting, we should do at least three things:

1. Ask ourselves, why is this meeting necessary? Be absolutely clear about the answer, and make sure everyone who attends understands as well.

2. Start on time. We penalize those who arrive on time by waiting for stragglers. No matter how important those stragglers may be, *all people* in attendance should be regarded as important; otherwise they wouldn't be there. On a spiritual level, one person's time is no less valuable than another's, no matter what the job title.

3. End on time. Let people know exactly how much time they're being asked to give. Once they've given it, don't try to take more.

The hard part of zen practice comes when we're called to a meeting that threatens to waste our time. Here we must learn the attitude zen masters call *muda zukai:* Making use of waste.

1. Keep an open mind. If we enter a room with a negative attitude, thinking we know everything that's going to transpire, we've closed ours mind to the possibility of learning. There is always something to learn, even if it has nothing to do with the point of the meeting.

2. Practice patience. Anxiousness and frustration result from wanting to be somewhere that we're not. We can only be where we are: Right here, right now. Zen practice is to accept that place with calm. We cannot always be master of the situation, but we can always be master of ourselves.

3. Contribute. Look for ways to make a positive contribution, in the same way a good musician knows how to jam in a group setting. We should avoid seeking to show off our chops—to demonstrate how much we know. We should seek what elevates the group as a whole.

4. Prepare for your turn. One day it will be your turn to lead the meeting. Watch; learn what works and what doesn't work. As the Japanese say, "An intelligent person who sees a weakness in another will correct the weakness in himself." It's easy to be critical from the sidelines; much harder to sit at the head of the table.

In every meeting, every moment offers a unique chance for enlightenment.

Don't waste it.

zen
business card

The exchange of business cards has long been standard practice in Japan, where it is customary for workers to identify themselves in terms of their company affiliation. The practice is now common in the West as well.

The Japanese word for business card, *meishi*, means literally, "the stab of name and fame." In other words, the intent of the card is to make a sharp, searing impression on the recipient.

Zen puts no quarter on fame, especially fame by association. Remove the title, the uniform, the trappings, and what do you have? A human being who will one day die, the same as everyone else. In zen, what matters is not our status but our spiritual development.

Along those lines, a zen story tells of a time the governor of Kyoto came to call upon the master Keichu. The governor presented his *meishi*, which read, "Kitagaki, Governor of Kyoto."

"I have no business with such a fellow," Keichu said. He instructed his attendant to turn the governor away.

The attendant returned the card, apologizing. The governor said, "No, that was my error." He then crossed out the words *Governor of Kyoto* and asked the attendant to try again.

"Oh, it's Kitagaki," Keichu said. "I want to see that fellow."

By crossing out his title, Kitagaki had chosen the humble path of zen. He came to Keichu not as a person of status, but as a fellow traveler of the Way—a human being.

The further we travel down the path of enlightenment, the more humble we become. We shouldn't seek to impress others—or allow ourselves to be taken—with mere outer trappings. If we do our inner work, our spirit will be our calling card.

Nice to meet you.

zen
Handshake

We shake hands so reflexively that we seldom stop to think what the custom signifies. It originated, anthropologists say, as a way for primitive people to show they were not carrying weapons.

In the Far East, where the custom is not to shake hands but to bow—an acknowledgment of the inherent deity in each other—the weaponless hand has powerful meaning as well. The name of the martial art *karate* translates as "empty hand." It signifies a form of self-defense that makes no use of weapons, only bare hands. The name also has spiritual meaning. Karate master Gichin Funakoshi says the ultimate aim of the art is for students to empty their hands, hearts, and minds of material desires, thereby reducing the prospect for conflict in the world.

As the most socially accepted means of touching, a handshake is one of the main ways we exchange energy with others. The next time you extend your hand, let your energy carry the message of Funakoshi's karate: That with an open hand goes an open heart and mind.

Peace.

zen
noon

zen
DRIVING

car
seat belt
road map
air conditioner
fuzzy dice
passenger
stop sign

zen car

The zen teacher Thich Nhat Hanh suggests that every time we start the car, we should reflect for a moment on what we're doing:

Before starting the car,
I know where I am going.
The car and I are one.
If the car goes fast, I go fast.

Nhat Hanh is not suggesting we give up our meandering Sunday drives. To say "I know where I am going" means we commit to following the spiritual path in front of us, wherever it leads. Even if we're driving down an unfamiliar street, we still "know where we're going" in a cosmic sense.

If we're racing down the road, it's often because our insides are racing rather than feeling calm. If we recognize our inherent oneness with the car—and, by extension, all things—we begin the process of slowing down inside, proceeding not in haste but under control.

We all know where we're going. There is only one final destination.

See you there.

zen seat belt

We do not proceed in life as though disaster is imminent. At the same time, we need to be aware of the potential for sudden, unpredictable change. Buckling our seat belt is an implicit acknowledgment that a crash might be out there. The zen attitude is to take nothing for granted. Just in case.

When we start taking things for granted, be it our health, safety, loved ones, or place in life, we inevitably fail to show proper gratitude for what we have.

So many of us take the gift of life for granted. Yet one inch ahead and all is total darkness. Life is precious; let's treat it so.

Buckle up and drive safely. Arrive alive, and give thanks.

That is zen.

zen road map

Every road we drive down, we're following the path of someone who has gone before. The same is true in zen.

We forget sometimes how much of our way has already been charted. All the highways, thoroughfares, and side streets we travel had to have been put there before we could drive them. Some are so old they grew out of footpaths from ages ago.

Likewise in zen, the road to enlightenment has been mapped out by the great sages of history. In Japan, the very word for teacher—*sensei*—means literally "previous in life" or "one who has gone before." As we make our way on the road of life, we rely on the *sensei* to guide us. When we start to stray, the *sensei* steers us back to the path. When we are confused at which way to turn, the *sensei* offers directions.

No matter who has paved the way for us, though, we all have to discover the truth for ourselves. Each of us is unique. No one has ever walked the exact path that we will walk, and no one can, because only we occupy this particular body in this particular space at this particular moment in time. Even with a road map in hand, we have to pay extra attention to every road sign when driving in a new city, because there is no teacher like our own experience.

Such was the lesson of the zen master Kempo, when a monk approached him asking for directions. The monk said, "It is written, 'All Buddhas enter the one straight road to Nirvana [unity with the absolute].' I still wonder where that road can be."

Kempo drew a line in the air with his staff. "Here it is," he said.

The one straight road stretches out before us, where all the sages have gone before.

Drive on.

zen
air conditioner

It's often said in the martial arts that the best training occurs in the hottest and coldest weather. Times like those are when the body learns to attune itself to nature's elements.

Likewise, there is no air conditioning or central heating in zen monasteries. Complaining about the temperature once, a monk asked his master, "How can we avoid these extremes?"

"Why not go where there is neither cold nor heat?" said the master.

"Is there such a place?" said the student.

"Certainly," the master said. "When cold, be thoroughly cold, and when hot, be thoroughly hot."

The master was saying, become one with the environment. We are in and of the environment, not separate from it; the temperature is not distinct from us. When there's no escaping the heat or the cold, the only way to combat it is to accept it.

Stay warm and keep cool—at the same time.

The moment you think it's hot as hell, remind yourself: "Here is heaven."

zen
FUZZY DICE

Fuzzy dice are decorations hung on rearview mirrors, typically by hot rod aficionados. They remind us that life is a game of chance. But so often we gamble foolishly when there is no need.

We see drivers passing others in a haste to get somewhere; nosing out other cars for a parking space; refusing other cars the room to change lanes. Tension increases. Road rage sets in. For what? So little is gained from such selfishness.

If angry drivers want to pass us in haste, let them. Where they're going is not the Way. Zen lies in saying, "After you." To act courteously and selflessly, to put the needs of others before our own, is to live with the compassion that blooms from true spiritual practice. As the *Tao Te Ching* says,

> *The sage is ahead*
> *by being behind;*
> *Is first*
> *by being last;*

Is whole
  by being empty;
And is fulfilled
  by being selfless.

Through the simple courtesy of saying, "After you," we begin to calm the mind and eliminate the feeling of rushing. We start to flow with the traffic, not fight it. "Flowing streams do not compete with one another," the zen masters say.

Leave those fuzzy dice where they are on the mirror. There is no need to roll them today.

Let someone else have a turn.

zen
passenger

Whenever we car-pool, ride the bus, or hop the train, we're passengers—traveling through time and space at the direction of a greater energy. But what is that energy?

The energy of the driver? The vehicle? The fuel that powers the vehicle? Or is it the divine?

No matter where we are, no matter where we go, we're all passengers on Mothership Earth, orbiting the sun at sixty thousand miles an hour.

Round and round we go.

Enjoy the ride.

zen
STOP SIGN

The stop sign reminds us to slow our pace, take a moment's rest, and look around. Therein lies a whole philosophy of life.

For all the rush of modern life, we need to remember the importance of stillness and quiet in spiritual practice. We should welcome those moments we can apply the brakes, take a deep breath, and gather ourselves before proceeding anew.

One of zen's great names, Ikkyu, means literally, "One Pause." Ikkyu received the name from his teacher upon breaking through to enlightenment. The decisive event that opened Ikkyu's mind was the cawing of a crow. What struck Ikkyu was not only the sound of the crow, but the pause between the sounds. As he later wrote of the experience,

one pause between each crow's
reckless shriek Ikkyu Ikkyu Ikkyu

To Ikkyu, the pause between shrieks symbolized the brief interval of human life. In the great chain of existence, we live on this earth for but one tiny pause, then it is time to move on.

Whether approaching an intersection or living in this interval: Make yours a full stop.

zen
LUNCH

drive-through
flag
burger
soda

zen
DrIVe-THrOUGH

Nothing epitomizes fast food better than the drive-through. Lunch to go without leaving your car! Our lives are so hurried today that we can't get the food fast enough.

But there's a zen element to the drive-through as well—the notion that everything we do and everywhere we go is part of one continuous path. As the zen masters say, *Kokon muni no michi:* "There is only one way."

We can stop and eat a leisurely lunch or fly through the drive-through, but there is only one way for us. We can't be doing anything other than what we're doing; when we're done, we move on. Every discreet event is part of a larger, 24/7 existence—one that continually carries forward.

Stopping, starting, driving through: It's all on the same path.

Everything to go.

zen flag

At the drive-through, we see the national and corporate flags atop the flagpole, flapping in the wind. But what, exactly, is moving?

A zen story tells of two monks debating just such a question. A flag had been hoisted outside a zen temple to announce the sermon of the master to the public. Upon seeing the flag blowing in the breeze, the first monk said, "The wind is moving." The other countered, "The flag is moving."

Upon hearing the argument, the zen master Bodhidharma corrected them both. "Not the wind, not the flag," he said. "Mind is moving."

All things in this world move as the earth turns on its axis around the sun. But through it all, zen teaches that we remain a still point at the center. If mind is moving, Bodhidharma says, we are not calm and centered. When we're calm and centered, the still point within moves as we move.

The wind has subsided, the flag lays limp.

Still
moving.

zen burger

Lunch is supposed to be a time to get out of the midday sun for some food before returning to work. But so often today we see busy people working through lunch or eating on the go. They walk down the street chomping on pizza or grab a burger at the drive-through and eat at their desk. There is a saying in zen, "Do not walk and eat at the same time." The same could be said for eating and working at the same time.

When the time comes to eat, even if just for a moment, sit, relax, and give thought to the food. It need not be a formal saying of grace, although many religious people begin that way. Just be mindful. Even those students and workaholics who seem to live on coffee and junk food can be thankful for the sustenance. Anyone who's ever gone hungry knows there is preciousness in all foods. Take nothing—not even a greasy plate lunch—for granted. That is spiritual living.

Some students mistakenly regard the saying "Do not walk and eat at the same time" as a hard-and-fast rule. But the point is simply to pay attention to one's actions. The zen teacher Seung Sahn offered a variation on this lesson at a retreat in San Francisco.

"Do not eat and read the newspaper at the same time," he said. "When you eat, just eat. When you read the newspaper, just read the newspaper."

The next morning, a student saw Sahn reading a newspaper while eating.

"I thought you said not to eat and read the newspaper at the same time," the student said.

To which Sahn replied, "When you eat and read the newspaper, just eat and read the newspaper."

And if you eat lunch on the run, then *eat lunch on the run*—aware of the doing and thankful you're here to do it.

Have it your way.

Have it the Way.

zen
soda

Pour a can of soda, and the fizz rises up out of the glass. That fizz is like our lives, zen masters say. In the words of the ancients, "When you boil rice, know that the water is your own life."

From the moment we open a can, we only have so long before the drink goes flat. Those bubbles that rise from a can of soda are so brief, so spirited, so effervescent—here and then gone—like us.

Drink up!

zen
errands

to-do list
bank deposit
ATM
dry cleaning
mall
shopping
credit card
signature
groceries

zen TO-DO LIST

Pay attention
Watch step
Stretch
Exercise
Wash the dishes
Wipe the mirror
Weed the garden
Do good work
Call Mom and Dad
Study
Practice
Follow through

zen Bank DeposIT

The future, zen masters tell us, is nothing but an illusion. All that exists is the present moment. So why save for tomorrow?

Because zen masters also say *shi on*–"think distant." It's true, zen is a philosophy of the present moment, but within the present moment lies the potential of the future. Every step we take in zen mixes an awareness of where we are on the path with an awareness of where we are stepping.

There are so many things we can do with our money instead of save it. But by setting some aside in savings, we engage in a conscious act of self-discipline. In so doing, we're not only "thinking distant," but practicing in the present moment.

Masters of the Japanese tea ceremony have a saying, "If there is preparation, there will be no regret." Prepare for the future in the present moment, and no matter what tomorrow brings, there will be no regret, because you will have taken the right step on the path.

A penny for your thoughts.

zen atm

Who doesn't want more money? We work for it, calculate how to borrow and spend it, fret over where to put it, dream of what it can do for us. We forget sometimes that spiritual riches matter more than material riches.

Materially, the world may be divided into haves and have-nots. But spiritually, we all inherently have. We need to stay open to that fact.

A zen parable makes that point in the tale of two friends, one of whom became more successful than the other. Wanting to help his poorer friend without embarrassing him, the richer man sewed a jewel into his friend's sleeve after the man fell asleep.

Later the man awoke, unaware of the jewel in his sleeve. As the years passed, he became more resentful of his friend's success. Finally, the richer man revealed the gift he had given: "I stitched a jewel into your sleeve, praying that it would give you the capital from which you might somehow make a living." Though his clothes were now tattered, the poor man looked in his sleeve to find the gift still there. That treasure became his salvation.

As the tea master Soshitsu Sen XV explains,

The jewel refers to the Buddha-nature within each of us. Although everyone possesses this treasure, most people are unaware of it. The man of standing who helped his friend to gain awareness represents the Buddha. The friend who lacked awareness of his friend's goodwill represents humanity. Not knowing of that treasure we all possess, our abilities are lost and we idle through a meaningless life.

If, as a function of living in the modern world, money is to dominate our thoughts, then let it be a meditation, not an obsession. When we take money from the cash machine, we should remember how we got that money—through toil, savings, and the charity of others—and give thanks for the treasure we all possess: The jewel in the sleeve.

Pocket your money and say, "I have what I need."

zen
DRY CLEANING

We tend to make distinctions in life between activities that are "important" and those that are not. Completing a major project on deadline is important; dropping off the dry cleaning is not. When we look back on the last year, we don't remember all the errands we ran, because what are we doing in running errands? Nothing in particular.

Therein lies zen.

The zen master Rinzai spoke glowingly of *bu ji:* Doing nothing. Literally, *bu ji* means "void of action" or "absence of action." Rinzai was not praising the merits of idleness. He was saying we should simply allow nature to take its course through us.

When a leaf falls from a tree, when a river flows to the sea, when a bee flits from flower to flower, it happens without "action" or "doing." Nature is simply being. In the same way, human beings should simply be, Rinzai says.

Intellectually, we may think *bu ji* is impossible to attain. On the contrary, it's completely natural to us. We don't always recognize *bu ji* because, by definition, when nature expresses itself through us, we're not conscious of "doing" anything. When we walk, we don't think about all the parts of our body working together to walk; we just walk. That is *bu ji:* Naturalness.

There are countless things we do during a day that seemingly have no significance, that we won't remember a year later or even a week later. Yet they're all part of living. Every mundane detail, quickly forgotten, marks our time on this earth. We're doing nothing.

Just living.

zen
maLL

With so many things to buy, the mall offers to satisfy needs we didn't even know we had. But how many of those things are absolutely vital? The very term *disposable income* suggests a use of money that's less than essential. Are we spending money just to acquire more things? Fulfill self-indulgent desires? Buy more than we can afford?

If we can reduce our desires, we automatically reduce our spending, leaving us more money for the things we deem essential. As the *Tao Te Ching* says,

The greatest misfortune
  is desire.
The greatest burden
  is greed.
The greatest curse
  is discontent.

Only those who know
  when enough is enough
  will ever have enough.

It's so easy to spend money, so easy to want things. A mall tends to make us focus on what we lack, rather than what we have. There's no doubt, shopping at the mall is fun. But when driven to make an impulse buy, look at what's driving the impulse. If desire, greed, and discontent are the cause, that's a signal to head home.

We won't find what we're looking for at the mall.

zen
SHOPPING

What money can buy	*What money can't buy*
Goods	Goodness
Services	Service
Food	Fulfillment
Books	Wisdom
Clothes	Style
Jogging shoes	Self-discipline
Art	Aesthetics
Gifts	Gratitude
Companies	Cooperation
Luxury	Grace
Face-lift	Youth
Land	Nature
Health care	Health
Political office	Character
Soldiers	Devotion
Guns	Security
Experiences	Experience
Zen	Zen

zen
CREDIT CARD

How quickly a credit card can send us spiraling down the financial sinkhole. The allure of "buy now, pay later" proves too tempting for many people to pass up, and suddenly the charges and interest create a pile of debt growing bigger by the month.

The Japanese say, "It's easier to find a thief on a mountain than it is to find a thief in your heart." The thief in our hearts is the desire for instant gratification: Wanting something without the means—or the discipline—to pay for it. We want the reward now, the pleasure now, the new toy now. We steal from our future to satisfy an immediate desire. We rob ourselves of money we've yet to even earn. Here is a thief we must find a way to apprehend.

Through zen, we learn the value of that which is hard-earned. When we've worked hard and saved our money toward a goal, we come to know how much that goal means to us in terms of time and effort. We may even realize the goal we once craved isn't so important anymore, that the money we sweated for should go to something more worthwhile.

Zen masters speak of the need for *nin,* which means "to silently endure." Literally, the word connotes "a sharp blade in the heart," a reference to the pain we bear through prolonged patience.

When reaching for the plastic without means to pay off the debt, wait. If it hurts to do so, use that sharp blade in the heart to kill the thief.

zen
signature

The zen master Dogen once said, "I am not other people, and other people are not me." A signature declares the same thing. It says, "I am this person and not someone else; this is my unique mark; this is what I'm willing to stand behind."

Whether signifying our agreement to pay the amount on a credit card slip, abide by the terms of a legal document, or accept authorship of a letter, a signature puts our name on the line, both literally and figuratively. Whatever we sign our name to, we have to take responsibility for.

Dogen says we have to take responsibility for our own enlightenment as well. To say "I am not other people, and other people are not me" means, I am the only one who can attain enlightenment in this body; no one else can do it for me. I must follow my own path and live with my decisions.

When signing a piece of paper, we'd do well to remember Dogen's words. As we write our name across the dotted line, let that line remind us of our commitment to follow the path.

Sign with the mind of accepting responsibility.

zen
Groceries

At the market, we pick through the fruits and vegetables and choose among cuts of fish and meat with an eye toward finding the best. But all foods bear the blessings of life.

That was the lesson the zen monk Banzo learned when he overheard a conversation between a butcher and his customer.

"Give me the best piece of meat you have," the customer said.

"Everything in my shop is the best," said the butcher. "You cannot find any piece of meat here that is not the best."

To Banzo's ears, the butcher was not merely boasting about the quality of his tenderloin. He was pointing to a deeper truth: All things have a divine radiance. There is nothing we can point to in the butcher shop—or the great wide world—that doesn't have it.

Put that radiance down on the grocery list, and remember to look for it.

zen workout

exercise
stretching
sit-ups
bicycle
jogging
water bottle
shower
toilet
munchies

zen
exercise

When doctors talk about the importance of exercise, they typically emphasize the physical benefits, but of course there are benefits to mind and spirit as well.

We build mental strength by overcoming the body's reluctance to exert itself. We all have excuses for not exercising—we don't have enough time, we're too tired, we'll start next week. It takes self-discipline to cut through those excuses and get the body moving. When we start to get lazy, the mind has to step in and focus attention. As the samurai say, "The only opponent is within." It's up to the mind to overcome the body's feelings of fatigue.

We continue to build mental focus by paying attention to the task at hand. Carrying the gym bag, changing into workout clothes, tying our shoelaces—every moment is an opportunity to keep the mind from laziness and wandering. The more we maintain focus, the more it carries over into everything we do, no matter how large or small the task.

Through the continued, willful exertion of effort, we sweat out our impurities and build a strong spirit—a willingness to overcome obstacles, a hunger to press on, a relentlessness on the path. The Japanese word for exercise, *undoh,* carries those very connotations. The word is rooted in the idea of an army on the move, pushing heavy equipment with strength and vigor. The first character of the word also has the meaning of "luck," suggesting the divine movement of fortune that accompanies a traveling army. Thus, inherent in *undoh* is the notion that, through self-exertion, we make our luck.

There are no excuses.

The only opponent is within.

zen
STRETCHING

The benefits of stretching before and after exercise are well documented. A limber body is less prone to injury and enables the body to move more fluidly. In the *Tao Te Ching* it says,

When people are born they are supple,
and when they die they are stiff.
When trees are born they are tender,
and when they die they are brittle.
Stiffness is thus a companion of death,
flexibility a companion of life.

We can apply those words not only to our bodies but to our minds as well. The more flexible our thinking, the more easy-going we become. Anytime we start to view the world rigidly, locked onto a track, we lose the flow that characterizes zen.

Here's an exercise to add while limbering up. When bending over to touch the toes, bow humbly to the earth. When stretching arms overhead, give praise to the sky.

That is stretching the mind.

zen
SIT-UPS

When the Japanese samurai wanted to knuckle down and make a serious effort at something, they would say, *Hara o kukuru:* "Tie the guts."

In doing sit-ups, we show the same resolve. The act of sitting up from flat on our back builds spiritual strength—pulling oneself up off the ground through a force of will. "Seven times down, eight times up," goes the Japanese adage. Whatever slips we make on the path, we have to get up and carry on. Sit-ups help build that kind of perseverance and character.

We sometimes think we need to join a health club or develop a workout routine before we can start exercising. But any spot on the floor will do for sit-ups—anytime, no matter where we are. We just have to get down on the ground and *tie the guts.*

zen
BICYCLE

Take the winner of the Tour de France and ask him how to ride a bicycle. No matter how knowledgeable he is, no matter how eloquent his words, nothing he can say will enable a beginner to simply get on a bike and go.

We learn about zen the same way we learn to ride a bicycle—through the experience of our own bodies. Theories and teaching can guide us, but zen lies in the doing; each of us has to find our own balance in order to ride a bicycle. Once we learn, we never forget, no matter how long we go without riding. "What you have been taught by listening to others' words you will forget very quickly," says the karate master Gichin Funakoshi. "What you have learned with your whole body you will remember for the rest of your life."

Through zen we seek to find and maintain that place of balance called *chudan,* meaning "middle ground." It is the ground of total balance, the place from which we wish to direct all our actions. When we move from our center, our center moves with us. Regardless of what we do or where we go, we stay rooted in the here and now.

Physically, mentally, and spiritually, we maintain our balance.

Like learning to ride a bicycle, finding such balance can be precarious. We can be knocked out of *chudan* in an instant. To achieve *chudan* takes practice. To maintain it takes even more.

If only it were so easy as to read a book on zen to gain enlightenment. A book can inspire us and offer insight, but no one can do the work of zen for us; each of us must take the initiative and seek the truth for ourselves. We must get on the bicycle, find our balance, and propel ourselves. Though we may fall down and skin our knees a few times, we have to get back on. There is no other way to learn.

Pedal on the one straight road ahead.

zen
JOGGING

One foot in front of the other foot in front of the other
foot in front of the other foot in front of the other foot in
front of the other foot in front of the other foot in front of
the other foot in front of the other foot in front of the
other foot in front of the other foot in front of the other
foot in front of the other foot in front of the other foot in
front of the other foot in front of the other foot in front of
the other foot in front of the other foot in front of the
other foot in front of the other foot in front of the other
foot in front of the other foot in front of the other foot in
front of the other foot in front of the other foot in front of
the other foot in front of the other foot in front of the
other foot in front of the other foot in front of the other
foot in front of the other foot in front of the other foot in
front of the other foot in front of the other foot in front of
the other foot in front of the other foot in front of the
other foot in front of the other foot in front of the other

zen
water bottle

A Chinese saying applies:

When you drink water, remember its source.

That's all there is to zen.

zen
shower

Every shower we take offers a moment of spiritual rebirth. As the water flows from above, running down our body, we feel revitalized by its energy. Our pores open and we rid ourselves of impurities. We wash, shedding our dead skin and buffing the new.

A shower subconsciously takes us back to the moment of our birth, when we emerge from the womb to an immediate cleansing. It offers a deep-seated sense of renewal, akin to what zen masters describe anytime we're too long away from water:

To feel the first rain
  after a long drought;
To come across an old friend
  in a foreign country.

Cleansed and newly born, we step from the shower and wrap ourselves in a towel.

Mother Earth waits with open arms.

zen
TOILET

We tend to think of the divine spirit in terms of radiance, but it encompasses all things, including the polluted, filthy, and vile.

Yes, zen can be found even in the toilet.

A monk once asked the zen master Ummon, "What is Buddha?"

The reply came, "A shit stick!"

The monk was shocked by the master's vulgarity. But Ummon's message was that all things speak of God, even soiled toilet paper. We may think of bodily waste as dirty, and yet it feeds the ground as fertilizer.

Another zen story tells of a student who asked his master, "Please show me zen."

The master said, "I have to go relieve myself."

Upon returning, the master said, "Zen is like going to the bathroom. I cannot go for you. You have to go for yourself."

Rich or poor, famous or anonymous: We all have to go.

When nature calls, listen to Nature.

zen
munchies

The horse in the field knows nothing of breakfast, lunch, or dinner. It eats when hungry. The point of zen is to follow that same kind of naturalness.

Zen masters have a saying, "Eat when hungry, sleep when tired." It means simply, listen to the rhythms of the body. The body has an inherent wisdom, telling us what it needs. If we ignore those needs too long, we weaken the vessel of our spirit.

Learning to distinguish between what the body needs and what it craves is part of training. For the true lesson of "Eat when hungry, sleep when tired" lies in what's unstated: Don't eat when not hungry. Don't overeat, indulge in too many cups of coffee, or use food as a substitute for emotional or spiritual sustenance.

"The biggest bowl fills last," zen masters say. Through reducing our cravings, we learn to keep our bowl small. Then it doesn't take much to satisfy our hunger.

When you grab a bite, make sure it's to feed your spirit.

zen
walk in the park

strolling
litter
blossom
cloud
rain
puddle
park bench

zen
STROLLING

More than any other part of the body, our feet keep us in touch with the earth. When we walk, zen masters say, we should take a moment to consider what's underfoot. "Walk as if you are kissing the Earth with your feet," says Thich Nhat Hanh. If we can move in that spirit, he says, "Every step makes a flower bloom."

The path of zen requires constant attentiveness, because we can lose the way so easily. The masters say, *Kyakka o miyo:* "Watch your step." A single act of laziness, selfishness, or mean-spiritedness can lead to a long detour from the path.

If we can proceed step by step, moving in balance, feet knowing their ground, then any direction we choose is the right way to go. No matter where we roam, we're on the royal road.

Step lively!

zen
LITTer

Zen masters have a saying, "Snowflakes do not fall on an inappropriate place." Neither does litter. A snowflake cannot fall anywhere but where it falls; where it lands is where it lands. The same is true for all things in this world, even a piece of trash in the park. If it is there, it reflects an expression of nature—in this case, someone's thoughtlessness or disregard. It is "appropriate" to the time and place because it emanates from human behavior. Everything is as it is in this moment, *because that's the way it is*.

Which is not to say the situation is unalterable. No one will give you credit for picking up someone else's litter— no one may even notice. But where there was ugliness, you restore beauty; where there was thoughtlessness, you show thoughtfulness.

Where snow fell before, a new snow falls to cover it up.

zen
BLOSSOM

In Japan, the cherry blossom has particular poetic meaning. The brevity and intensity of the bloom serves as a metaphor for our short time on this earth. As the poet Basho wrote,

Between our two lives
there is also the life of
the cherry blossom

We needn't dwell on that brevity, though; all that matters is that the flower is in bloom.

Like each and every one of us.

Every flower contains the message and mystery of life. The Buddha twirled a flower, and Kasyapa smiled. The Buddha could have held anything in his hand, and the message would have been the same. But he held a flower.

Look deeply into that flower, says the tea master Sen Rikyu, for it tells a universal story. Legend has it that the shogun of Japan, Toyotomi Hideyoshi, once visited Rikyu to see some morning glories, which at the time were a rarity in Japan. The shogun arrived, expecting a profusion of fresh flowers, but saw nothing as he approached the house. Disappointed, he entered the tearoom. In the decorative alcove he spied a single morning glory, floating in a container, wet with dew.

Rikyu's message: Look at the beauty of this one flower. There, in the story of just one flower, is the story of all life: The inherent energy that brought it to bloom; the radiance of the moment; the withering to come; and the seed of rebirth. That is the truth of nature, and of us as well.

If the shogun had seen a field of morning glories, they would have looked beautiful, but indiscriminate. By showing just one, Rikyu brought out the uniqueness of the flower and the beauty of all morning glories—and, by extension, the beauty of all things on this earth in their glorious, individual diversity.

Of all the things in this vast, wide world, the Buddha held a single flower.

Stop and smell—and smile.

zen
CLOUD

As children, we look up at the clouds and imagine seeing different shapes—a rabbit, a lion, a dragon. In zen, we see the spiritual significance of the clouds.

All we need to know about our time on this earth is to look up at the sky and see the clouds. Pick a cloud, any cloud. It is the picture of your spirit.

Zen refers to its wandering monks as *unsui,* literally, "cloud and water." To be an *unsui* is to embody the spirit of zen training, floating, flowing, at once with and without form. A cloud is here before our eyes, ever changing, evolving through a vast canvas of emptiness, and then it is gone, like ourselves.

Every day, the silent sky speaks the dynamic truth, plain for all to see.

One cloud tells the story.

zen
rain

When zen masters say, "Every day is a good day," they include the weather, too.

We often make distinctions between "good weather" and "bad weather," but what's good weather for one person is bad weather for another. Somewhere, a farmer is praying for rain. Somewhere else, a picnic-goer is praying for blue skies. Such is always the case. A zen poem says,

The prayed-for rain
Fell on those who
Didn't want it.

Whatever the day's weather, we have to accept it. To complain about the rain, or lack of it, shows a mind out of tune with nature. Align with nature, and, rain or shine, the weather is always welcome. Without the rain, without the sun, there would be no bloom in spring, no life on earth.

Let a smile be your umbrella.

zen
PUDDLE

After the rain falls, zen lies in the puddles.

If we look down at a puddle, we can see the reflection of a passing cloud overhead. No matter which puddle we choose, we will see the same cloud. All the myriad things in the world are like those puddles, zen masters say, each one reflecting the same thing. Every puddle has a different shape and size, but no matter how small around or how shallow, the reflection doesn't vary. As a zen saying goes,

One moon shows in every pool;
In every pool, the one moon.

If we return to the same spot after the sun has shone for a while, the puddle will be gone—evaporated into the clouds above.

Now the passing cloud casts its shadow on the cake of dirt left behind.

zen
park bench

A park bench is good place to watch the world go by, to enjoy the variety and spectacle of life around us. It's also a place to be alone with our thoughts. Zen students sometimes fall into the trap of navel gazing—that is, looking inward to the point of becoming self-absorbed. We forget that the navel should lead our mind outward, not inward.

All of us were born of a mother, connected physically by an umbilical cord, just as she was connected to her mother. Back and back the cord goes, to the origin of all being.

If we're going to make a meditation of our belly button, let's remember that cord. It's still there, connecting us to all who pass through the great parade of life.

Behold your family walking by.

zen
moon

zen
DInner

cooking
kitchen knife
disposal
dinner table
candle
dessert

zen
cooking

Japanese cooking uses a lot of soy sauce, French cooking uses a lot of butter, Italian cooking uses a lot of garlic. No matter what the style of cooking, though, the most important ingredient never varies: the love put in by the cook.

Masters of the Japanese tea ceremony use the term *kokoro ire,* or "inclusion of the heart's spirit." The best tea ceremonies have nothing to do with fancy surroundings or making a good impression; the determinant of success is the sincere and humble heart of the host.

I once had a musician friend invite me over for dinner. I was unaware he had so little money he could barely afford to buy food. The entire meal consisted of carrots and rice—and it was delicious. Never had I truly *tasted* carrots and rice before that moment. The depth of his *kokoro ire* gave the meal an unforgettable flavor.

Heart is what separates good cooking from the idea of food as mere fuel. If people regard cooking as a duty or a chore, the meal will lack spirit. If they cook timidly, unsure of their taste, the result will be bland. If they try too hard to make something delicious, the food will taste overwrought. If they feel pressured to serve on time, the haste will show on the plate.

Whatever we set out to make—a meal, a table, a bed— we should make as well as we can. To do otherwise is spiritless.

Cook boldly. Serve your heart, and what's empty will be filled.

zen
KITCHEN KNIFE

Chopping the vegetables and carving the turkey remind us of the zen saying, "The sword cannot cut itself."

Zen masters use the saying as a warning against trying to understand the truth through rational means. In the same way that a knife can be used to cut anything but its own blade, we can use logic to analyze human problems, but we cannot arrive at enlightenment through deduction. Our thinking may be razor sharp and our will like tempered steel, but mere logic can never understand the divine mind. The truth lies inside each and every one of us, but we can't extract it through thinking.

But if the truth lies inside, how can we extract it?

Chop the vegetables, carve the turkey.

zen
DISPOSaL

A friend once told me he believed in "stealth cooking." I asked what he meant.

"When you're done," he said, "there should be no evidence you were ever in the kitchen."

His attitude mirrors what the zen masters say: "Polish your path." Some cooks prepare their meals and leave a big mess for later, but the way of zen is to clean as you go. Rinse things down, run the disposal, and put ingredients away *as part of the process* of cooking. We can apply that attitude to everything we do, be it housework or living in the environment at large.

In such a way is cleanliness next to zenliness.

zen
DINNER TABLE

In many homes, the evening's meal is a time to come together with family, friends, or loved ones and linger in one another's company. When we gather to eat, we take sustenance not only in breaking bread and sharing wine, but also in each other. What we take from those meals binds us together and sustains our collective spirit.

Even in dining solo, we need not feel alone. The divine presence is always there. If we partake in each meal with gratitude, there is sharing going on between ourselves and Great Nature. Make room for the spirit of Buddha at your dinner table.

"A person who is eating has neither greed nor anger," goes a zen saying. The partaking of food promotes a harmony within ourselves, as well as with nature and those with whom we share our meal. From the small harmony of a meal at day's end grows the larger harmony of the family, the community, and all that surrounds.

Dinner is served.

The whole world is seated.

zen
candle

Light a candle at dinner, and a small flame casts divine light over the meal, providing quiet warmth and a reminder of nature's energy.

We compare our time on this earth to that of a candle, growing shorter with each day. But through zen we come to identify ourselves as not the candle, but the flame. When the candle burns out, the flame may vanish—but only until the next match is lit. As an elemental force, fire simply *is,* an energy inherent to the air.

A gust of wind, the flame is gone.

Where did it go?

zen
dessert

Dessert can often be an indulgence. But a good chef will offer just the right dessert as the coup de grâce of a fine meal, a treat to nestle in a corner of the stomach the diner didn't even know was there. Such desserts can be savored long after the meal has ended.

If only we could learn to savor life the same way. The Buddha makes that very point in a parable about a man running from a tiger. The man reaches a precipice and grabs hold of a root, swinging over the edge. Down below, he sees a second tiger waiting.

Suddenly, two mice, one white and one black, start gnawing at the vine. Clinging for his life, the man spies a strawberry growing on a vine nearby. He plucks it and puts it in his mouth:

"How sweet the taste!"

The Buddha's lesson: Do not wait for the moment of imminent death to taste life's sweetness. Savor it now. Every breath we take is precious. Treat it as such, and all of life becomes a luscious dessert.

We *can* have our cake and eat it, too.

zen
chores

garbage
dishwashing
sweeping
laundry

zen
Garbage

Spiritual practice demands attention to our actions, even in throwing out the garbage. A student of the zen master Gisan attained enlightenment in one moment of waste.

When Gisan asked the student to bring a pail of water for his bath, the student poured it in and threw the remainder on the ground. The master scolded him: "Why didn't you give the rest of the water to the plants? What right have you to waste even a drop of water in this temple?"

In that instant, the student realized zen. To signify his spiritual rebirth, he took the name Tekisui, meaning "a drop of water."

I had a similar awakening once while throwing out the trash in New York City. On the nights before trash collection, it's typical for homeless people to walk the streets riffling through newly deposited bags to look for food scraps. On this particular night, I had emptied my cat's litter box into the trash along with garbage from the kitchen. I returned later that evening to find a homeless person sorting through the bag I had thrown out. "Why

do people put their cat litter in here!" he said. "All this food is ruined!"

I realized then that not all garbage is equal—or even garbage. That just because something is no longer useful to me doesn't make it useless. And that I should pay attention not only to what I discard, but also to how I throw it away.

We can have the trash hauled out of sight, but in zen, not out of mind.

zen
DISHWASHING

One of zen's most famous stories involves a lesson the zen master Joshu gave to a new monk in training.

"I have just entered the monastery," the monk said. "Please teach me."

"Have you eaten your rice porridge?" Joshu asked.

"Yes," said the monk.

"Then you had better wash your bowl."

Joshu's lesson is simple, yet profound: Follow through.

Every moment is at once distinct and part of a continuous line. To walk that line in zen means continuing through to the next moment. When the meal is over, we wash the dishes; when the dishes are clean, we put them away. Zen is nothing more than adhering to such simple tasks, *with full attention*. If we pay attention to what we're eating, the way we clean up, and where we put things, we won't need to ask for spiritual instruction.

We'll be giving it.

zen
SWEEPING

It's safe to say the technology of brooms hasn't changed much over the centuries. People have been sweeping the floor for as long as dust has gathered.

The human need to sweep reflects more than a longing for cleanliness. The act grows out of our inherent spirituality, zen masters say.

"Such actions as clearing the dust from the room and the dead leaves from the garden path all represent clearing the 'dust of the world,' or the worldly attachments, from one's heart and mind," says the tea master Soshitsu Sen XV. "The act of cleaning thus enables one to sense the pure and sacred essence of things, man, and nature."

The Buddha tells of a time he met a man named Sri, whose brother had given up on trying to educate him. Thinking himself dumb, Sri tearfully told the Buddha how he had tried to become learned but could not remember a thing.

The Buddha handed him a broom and dustbin, saying, "Every day, sweep and clean. Remove all the dust of the world."

Through repeating that one simple practice, Sri attained enlightenment.

Whenever we clean our surroundings, we feel refreshed inside. Zen is nothing more than repeating that practice day after day.

One day at a time.

One clean sweep.

zen
Laundry

It never ends.

There is always more laundry to do.

There will always be more laundry to do.

Daily, we work and dirty our clothes with sweat. We throw them in the laundry and repeat the process again the next day.

A continuous cycle of toil, soil, and cleaning.

Sounds like zen.

zen
downtime

living room
beer
TV
movie
music
reading

zen
LIVING room

A martial arts training hall is called a *dojo*. Literally, *dojo* means "place of the Way," a reference to the great Way of nature and life. Through our actions in the *dojo,* we seek to align ourselves with the Way.

Any place can be a *dojo*. All that's required is the proper frame of mind. I have seen martial arts classes held in garages, parking lots, and cafeterias. No matter what the surroundings, the students still bow when they arrive and depart, in deference to the teacher and the spiritual nature of their activity.

Just as religious adherents do not need a church, temple, or synagogue to pray, neither do zen students need a monastery to lead a zen life. So long as your spirit is right, any and every room can be a place of practice. As zen masters say, "The Way is wherever people discipline themselves through training."

In the kitchen, prepare your food with zest and attention.

In the dining room, receive your food with gratitude and delight.

In the bathroom, cleanse yourself of the dust of the world.

In the bedroom, let go of the day and take your rest.

In the living room, live.

zen
beer

One generally doesn't associate zen with beer. After all, monks follow a strict ascetic regiment. But zen monks are different from zen itself. While monks may follow a teetotaling line, zen encompasses both the drinker and the dry.

The history of Eastern religion contains many examples of spiritual leaders who liked to imbibe. The Sixth Dalai Lama, Tsangyang Gyatso, is best remembered for his love of bars and women:

> *If the bar girl does not falter,*
> *The beer will flow on and on.*
> *This maiden is my refuge*
> *And this place my haven.*

As with all things in zen, the path to the truth lies in the Middle Way between opposites. If we drink, we have to know our limit. If we refrain, we should not judge those who partake. The paths to enlightenment are myriad; those who claim there is only one way are blind to the truth themselves.

A zen story makes that point by telling of two teachers with opposing philosophies. The first, Unsho, never drank. The second, Tanzan, enjoyed wine.

One day Unsho visited Tanzan, who was drinking at the time.

"Won't you have a drink?" Tanzan asked.

"I never drink," Unsho said.

"One who does not drink is not even human," Tanzan said.

Incredulous, Unsho said, "Do you mean to call me inhuman just because I do not indulge in wine? If I'm not human, what am I?"

"A Buddha," Tanzan said.

Eat, drink, and be merry.
Or just eat and be merry.
Either way, cheers.

zen TV

Watching television is another activity that would seem to be the antithesis of zen practice. Where zen asks that we empty our minds, television fills us with sounds and pictures. Where zen says to release the mind from attachments, television sells us the new and improved attachment. Where zen says to let the mind abide no place, television fixates our attention on the screen. We've become so accustomed to a life of stimuli that we seem afraid to just sit in a room with our own thoughts.

And yet . . .

Zen encompasses all things—even television. Sure, you joke, the zen of television is easy to see: The blank screen of a TV that's turned off. But even when on, television offers the same opportunity for enlightenment as any other activity, so long as we watch mindfully and not mindlessly. When we turn on the TV, it should be with awareness of what we're doing, even if all we want is a little escapism, to unwind from the pressures of the day and take the mind away from fixating on a problem.

Be it drama, sitcom, game show, talk show, the news, or an ad, whatever appears on the air is broadcast in order to be seen. Thus, at bottom, everything on the air carries the same underlying message: *Watch this, and stay tuned.* Is that not a zen message?

Watch this: Pay attention. Focus right here, right now. Absorb yourself in this moment.

Stay tuned: Keep body, mind, and spirit in tune—that is, in harmony. Maintain harmony within and without, in this moment and into the next.

How we respond to television's underlying message says a lot about our values and behavior. Either we choose to watch and stay tuned, or we don't. What do we think is worthy of our attention? What we will give our precious time on this earth to watch? It may be a weeklong miniseries or a moment's image on the screen as we're channel surfing. What is it that captures our attention, however long or fleetingly? Conversely, why do we surf past certain images or ignore one program in favor of another? Why do we allow the set to remain on while we're complaining, "There's nothing good on TV"? The more we answer those questions, the more mindful we become of what we're doing and why.

Without question, we should keep the hours of television viewing to a minimum. Zen demands the self-discipline to know when enough is enough. Even the moment of clicking off offers a chance for realization, as one feels the emptiness created in a room suddenly gone silent. What fills the space?

The blank screen, too, says, *Watch this, and stay tuned.*

zen movie

The zen masters of old never saw a movie, but they would certainly understand the film medium if they did. Zen teaches that this world of time and space—what we call reality—is an illusory veil that masks the source of a timeless, spaceless eternity. In that sense, life is like a movie projected onto a giant screen. The projector is a Great Void, from which all things emanate.

The sage Chuang-Tzu described the experience as akin to a multi-level illusion: "I dreamed I was a butterfly dreaming I was a man," he said. Zen masters sum up the experience by saying, *Mu-ichi-motsu:* Not a "thing" exists. We take our body, this chair, and this table to exist, but zen says, ultimately, they are apparitions—part of the great shadowplay called life.

In the same way that a great movie draws us in, eliciting an emotional investment in the outcome, so, too, does life make us care about the characters and the story. On a philosophical level, not a "thing" may exist, but we play our role to the hilt nonetheless.

In the movie called life, we're the stars.

Action!

zen music

Before the advent of recording machines, the only way to enjoy music was to play it or hear it performed live. Thanks to modern technology, we can now enjoy our favorite songs wherever we go, whenever we want.

The recordings we play are exactly that: Documents of a particular moment in time. Those recordings contain a spirit ready for release at any time. The key to that spirit— what makes good music—is what the Chinese call *ch'iyun:* a "sympathetic vibration of the vital spirit." *Ch'iyun* connects the heart of the musician to the heart of the listener, creating a spiritual harmony across space and time. Years after the artist's death, the *ch'iyun* captured in a single recording can carry on, transporting listeners to a higher place, changing the lives of people the artist never knew.

What gives *ch'iyun* that special vibration? The great rhythm at our core, the energy that drives the dance of life. Zen masters call it *sekishu no onjo:* "the sound of one hand clapping."

Call it is the sound of emptiness, the sound of silence, or the voice of God. Whatever you call it:

Move to the rhythm and dance.

zen
reaDInG

There is no disputing the power of books. Witness the book burnings in totalitarian states or the efforts to ban certain books from school libraries. Books have the capacity to unleash uncontrollable forces both liberating and dangerous. "One lash to a bright horse, one word to a wise man," goes a zen saying. One book can change the course of history.

On the path of enlightenment, the sages of yesteryear continue to teach and show us the Way. We all have to discover the truth for ourselves, but the great books are there to inspire and guide us.

In typical zen paradox, some of those very same works warn against the written word. The only book we ever need, they say, is the one with no words:

The wind is soft, the moon is serene.
Calmly I read the True Word of no letters.

Zen masters worry that we can become too attached to words and books. Some go as far to say that books should be burned—but only *after they're read and committed to heart*. What matters is not to have a book, they say, but to know what it says. How many times have we finished a book and, a short while later, forgotten the book's message?

A zen story warns against clinging to even the most cherished of books:

On his deathbed, the master Mu-nan called his disciple, Shoju, into his room.

"Here is a book," he said. "It has been passed down from master to master for seven generations. I also have added many points according to my understanding. The book is very valuable, and I am giving it to you to represent your successorship."

"If the book is such an important thing, you had better keep it," Shoju said. "I have received your zen without writing and am satisfied with it as it is."

"I know you have," the master said, "but here, you should keep this as a symbol of the teaching." He forced it into Shoju's hand.

Shoju accepted the book and laid it on the flaming coals of the brazier.

"What are you doing!" Mu-nan shouted.

"What are you saying!" Shoju replied.

Unlike most acts of book burning, which stem from a fear of knowledge, Shoju's act showed a level of enlightenment. In burning Mu-nan's book, he taught his own teacher a lesson: Let go. Nothing material lasts forever, least of all this material body we inhabit. There is nothing in your book I do not know—nor can there be, once enlightenment is attained. As for passing the book on to future generations, no written word can give them the experience of enlightenment.

In the ultimate nature of the universe, all books and all writing vanish into nothingness. As the zen master Ikkyu wrote,

Writing something
To leave behind
Is yet another kind of dream:
When I awake I know that
There will be no one to read it.

Fix those words in your heart and you can set this very book on fire.

zen
BEDTIME

moonlight
star
crickets
laughing
sex
bed
sleep
dream

zen moonlight

In zen literature, no metaphor is more popular than the moon. With its beauty, cycles, reflected light, and availability to all, the moon symbolizes nature's great truth.

A zen verse says,

The servant asks me
  [life's] deepest
  meaning:
Smiling, I point outside
  the silk-curtained window
  —the autumn moon.

All of zen teaching is like a finger pointing to the moon. Everything the masters say and do is intended to show the way to the beautiful light in the sky. Don't concentrate on the finger, teachers say, because the finger only points the way. Likewise, zen teaching is merely a *guide* to the truth, not the truth itself. Focus on the glory of the moon. There is where the truth lies.

Such was the lesson of the zen master Ryokan Daigu, who returned home one night to find a thief in his hut.

Living an ascetic life, Ryokan had nothing worth stealing. Nevertheless, he told the intruder, "You may have come a long way to visit me, and you should not return empty-handed. Please take my clothes as a gift." He took the shirt off his back and gave it to the man.

The thief took the clothes and ran.

Gazing up at the evening sky, Ryokan said, "Poor fellow. I wish I could give him this beautiful moon." Later, he wrote in verse,

The thief left it
There in the windowframe—
The shining moon.

So many of us are like that thief—consumed with material possessions, clinging to things, grabbing for more, hoarding attachments, and oblivious to the eternal truth. Zen asks us to consider,

Does the moon
Slip by
With no intention?
It's a messenger warning
That your life is passing.

One cycle finishes and another begins. Holding nothing, we mirror the light of the universe.

The truth is right there in the sky before us.

zen
star

As children we learn to sing,

Twinkle, twinkle, little star
How I wonder what you are

Through generations, the song endures because it is simple, innocent, and true, evoking the eternal mystery of the universe. Where there is wonder, there is zen—like a diamond in the sky.

May wonder never cease.

zen crickets

Listen to the dark.

Hear those crickets?

Therein lies enlightenment.

That is the teaching of *Jugyu-zu,* or "Ten Bull-Herding Pictures," offered by the twelfth-century zen master Kakuan. *Jugyu-Zu* likens our inner struggle for enlightenment to that of a herder trying to rein in a bull, where the bull represents the eternal principle of nature in action. With each advance the herder makes in harnessing the bull, he moves closer to the ultimate realization of zen.

In the beginning, Kakuan says, the herder cannot even locate the bull:

Wherever he seeks, he can find no trace,
no clue. Exhausted and in despair,
As the evening darkens he hears only the
crickets in the maples.

The herder is in a deeply confused state, desperately wanting to find his True Nature, that essential vibrancy that energizes all things in the universe, but he doesn't know where to look. So many of us are like that herder—

unhappy, roaming the world in search of the Answer. Yet we never stop to look right where we stand.

If, like the herder, we're exhausted and despairing, the time has come to rest. *Listen to the crickets,* Kakuan says. If we meditate on that one sound long enough, we begin our way out of confusion and back onto the path. One sound can be our guide. Enlightenment awaits anyone with ears enough to hear it.

For the herder of Kakuan's tale, the sound of crickets is what eventually leads him on the trail to finding the bull. In succeeding stages, he is able to move deeper and deeper inside himself until realizing the ultimate truth.

Stop.
Listen.
The way to the truth begins with the sound of crickets.

zen
LAUGHING

If someone were to ask, "What is zen?" the best answer might be a laugh—not a fake "ha-ha" laugh, but a spontaneous laugh from the belly. When laughter arises without any conscious thought, that is zen—a completely natural reaction to the moment. When we have to explain the punch line to someone who doesn't get it, the humor is gone—and so is the zen.

Zen has the impression of being serious and severe, but as a philosophy that uses paradox to get at the truth, it often finds humor in the absurd. Take, for example, the following exchange between two monks:

"I am going to ask you a question," said the first. "Can you answer?"

"What's the question?"

"I already asked it."

"Well, I already answered it."

"What did you answer?"

"What did you ask?"

"I asked nothing," said the first.

"And I answered nothing," said the second.

Zen embraces even those who laugh at zen. As the *Tao Te Ching* says,

> *When lesser people hear of the Way,*
>   *they ridicule it greatly.*
> *If they didn't laugh at it,*
>   *it wouldn't be the Way.*

Laugh at the Way, laugh with the Way.
Laughter *is* the Way.

zen
sex

Zen monks renounce sex, calling it an earthly desire to be transcended. But the zen master Ikkyu saw sex as the gateway to enlightenment:

The autumn breeze of a single night of love is
better than a hundred thousand years of
sterile sitting meditation . . .

In Ikkyu's zen, sex connects us directly to the source of creation. All of us are born of a man and woman, he said. We're *of* sex, a fact that should be embraced, not avoided. We, like our partners, are manifestations of the divine. Sex should have a sacred, even prayerful, dimension at the same time as being great fun.

All we need do is simply *make love* in the deepest sense of those words. As stated before, whatever we set out to make, we should make as best as we can. The same rule applies in making love. Put your whole spirit into the *making*. Sometimes we neglect our partner or put forth a half-hearted effort. Great sex is a full body, full mind, full *spirit* experience. If our whole heart isn't involved, we're not making love, we're making a mess of things.

True love-making ripples out into the surrounding world. It can take physical form, in the making of a child that grows into a healthy, caring member of society. Or it can manifest itself spiritually. When two lovers tap into the source of creation, the glow that results carries forward and spreads to all whom they meet.

From one act of love, ten thousand lives feel the blessing. Now that's really *love*-making.

zen
BED

On one level, masters tell us, zen is nothing more than "walking, standing, sitting, lying." Those are the four basic positions of the human body. "Walking, standing, sitting, lying" suggests that, no matter what the body is doing, we maintain a zen attitude. Beyond that, "walking, standing, sitting, lying" describes our progression in life:

In the early going, we walk along the path of life, searching, experiencing, and growing.

As we mature, we stand and establish our ground.

As we reach life's end, we sit in contemplation.

At the end, we expire and take our final posture— lying in the grave.

When the day is over and it's time to retire, let us walk to our beds, knowing the path we took to get there; stand and disrobe, shedding our outer skin from the day; sit and reflect on what we've learned; then lie down in peace.

We have reached our resting place.

zen
sleep

Try as we might to outlast it, sleep catches up with every one of us. "It conquers the tiger, it conquers the lion, and it conquers the enraged bull," goes a saying. "It conquers men and kings. They all fall, overcome, at its feet."

Some people go down fitfully, their minds racing with problems until they drift off in exhaustion. Others go down easily, welcoming the end of the day. Zen lies in the peaceful release of the latter. "Just go to sleep," the masters say. That in and of itself is living naturally.

A zen story says as much when it tells of two monks who spoke after spending the summer away from the monastery.

"What did you do over the summer?" asked the first monk.

"I plowed a field and sowed a basket of seeds," said the second.

"That's good, you didn't waste your time."

"And what did you do?" the second monk asked.

"During the day I ate, and at night I slept," said the first.

"That's good. You didn't waste your time, either."

If we truly live the philosophy of "one day, one life-time," we come to see each sleep as both an end and a beginning—the end of the day just past and the beginning of the day to come. Moreover, we begin to equate the inevitability of sleep with the inevitability of death. We realize that both are natural and unavoidable occurrences.

Today was a good day.
And now, good night.

zen dream

This day—
a dream.

This self—
a dream.

This life—
a dream.

This dream—
a dream.

Awaken.

ABOUT THE ILLUSTRATIONS

The illustrations in this book were created by Bo Hok Cline, design director for Netscape. I first encountered her work when, to accompany an MSNBC.com excerpt of my book *Zen Computer,* she used Japanese-style brush strokes to create a beautiful, contemporary image of a computer. I asked if she would consider applying that same style to the content of *Zen 24/7.* To my great delight, she accepted. The book is all the richer for it.

SELECT BIBLIOGraPHY

Berg, Stephen. *Crow with No Mouth: Ikkyu, 15th Century Zen Master.* Port Townsend, WA: Copper Canyon Press, 1989.

Cleary, Thomas. *The Essential Tao.* New York: Castle Books, 1998.

Deng Ming-Dao. *Zen: The Art of Modern Eastern Cooking.* San Francisco: SOMA Books, 1998.

Funakoshi, Gichin. *Karate-Do: My Way of Life.* Tokyo: Kodansha International, 1975.

Grigg, Ray. *The New Lao Tzu: A Contemporary Tao Te Ching.* Boston: Charles E. Tuttle, 1995.

Lao Tzu. *The Way of Life: A New Translation of the Tao Te Ching.* Translated by R. B. Blakney. New York: Mentor, 1955.

Musashi, Miyamoto. *The Book of Five Rings.* Translated by Nihon Services Corporation. New York: Bantam Books, 1982.

Nakamura, Tadashi. *One Day, One Lifetime: An Illustrated Guide to the Spirit, Practice, and Philosophy of Seido Karate Meditation.* New York: World Seido Karate Organization, 1992.

Nhat Hanh, Thich. *Peace Is Every Step.* New York: Bantam Books, 1991.

Reps, Paul. *Zen Flesh, Zen Bones.* New York: Anchor Books, 1961.

Sekida, Katsuki. *Two Zen Classics: Mumonkan and Hekiganroku.* New York: Weatherhill, 1977.

Shigematsu, Soiku, trans. *A Zen Forest: Sayings of the Masters*. New York: Weatherhill, 1981.

Shimano, Eido Tai, and Kogetsu Tani. *Zen Word, Zen Calligraphy*. Boston: Shambhala, 1990.

Soshitsu Sen XV. *Tea Life, Tea Mind*. New York: Weatherhill, 1979.

Stevens, John, trans. and ed. *Wild Ways: Zen Poems of Ikkyu*. Boston: Shambhala, 1995.

Sudo, Philip Toshio. *Zen Computer: Mindfulness and the Machine*. New York: Simon & Schuster, 1999.

———. *Zen Guitar*. New York: Simon & Schuster, 1997.

———. *Zen Sex: The Way of Making Love*. San Francisco: HarperSanFrancisco, 2000.

The Venerable Myokyo-ni. *Gentling the Bull: The Ten Bull Pictures, a Spiritual Journey*. Boston: Charles E. Tuttle, 1988.

ACKnOWLEDGMENTS

Thanks go to:

My gem of an agent, Laurie Fox of Linda Chester and Associates, for her unwavering support and enthusiasm;

My editor, Doug Abrams, for helping to shape the book and caring so much about every page;

Renee Sedliar, for her careful attention to both the words and their production;

And all the folks at Harper San Francisco, who've given of themselves to bring this book into the world.

Thanks also to:

Bo Hok Cline, for being open to the job and creating the perfect illustrations;

Salvatore Principato, for believing in the project in the moment of doubt;

My parents and brothers, for being behind me;

Naomi, Keith, and Jonathan, for being who you are;

and Tracy, for being.

AUTHOR CONTACT

The author welcomes comments, questions, and inquiries via e-mail at:

psudo@zencomputer.com

or via regular mail at:

P.O. Box 385278
Minneapolis, MN 55438

Read material from the author's other works and join the community of fellow readers at:

www.zenguitar.com

www.zencomputer.com

www.zensex.org